JEFFREY ALLEN'S GUIDE TO KARAOKE CONFIDENCE

ISBN 0-7604-0007-5

9 780760 400074

For Kimberley,
Nicole and Jacqueline...

CONSULTING EDITOR
Sandy Feldstein
President, Chief Operating Officer
Warner Bros. Publications Inc.

CO-ORDINATING EDITOR
Diane Laucirica

DESIGN AND LAYOUT
Susan Hartline Long

EDITED
by Cathy J. Moulton
Anthony J. Allen

INSTRUCTIONAL DRAWINGS
by Kimberley Allen

PHOTOGRAPHY
by Mitch Tobias

COVER DESIGN
by Kimberley Allen

TABLE OF CONTENTS

INTRODUCTION

PART 1: SECRETS OF LIVING COMFORTABLY ONSTAGE

TABLE OF CONTENTS

PART 2: THE VOCAL MAKEOVER: TRICKS, TIPS AND SECRETS OF SINGING

SETTING THE STAGE FOR EXPRESSIVE SINGING

FIGURE 2

INTRODUCTION

Nightclubs, hotels and living rooms the world over may never be the same. The Japanese singing phenomenon commonly known as Karaoke is infiltrating popular culture around the world in a big way. Karaoke (literally translated as "empty orchestra") is commonly pronounced carry-OH-key whereas the common Asian pronunciation is closer to kah-rah-OH-kay.

With Karaoke bars and clubs popping up in virtually every cosmopolitan city, "Just get up there and sing!" can be heard night after night as average non-singing adults grab their 3½ minutes in the spotlight.

Bankers, nurses, car mechanics, stockbrokers, lawyers, truck drivers, secretaries and individuals from every walk of life are discovering there is no better way to have fun on Saturday night (or any other night for that matter), than to sing for a captive audience.

Singing unlike any other activity gets the juices flowing. The microphone is the ultimate equalizer: no one is immune to nervousness, jeopardy of failure or outright joy of an appreciative audience after a good sing.

Karaoke nightclubs are also great places where singers with dreams of grandeur can benefit from the exposure of singing in front of a live audience. Amateurs can simply have fun or hone their vocal skills, while professionals can give their instruments and performing know-how a tune-up.

Through Karaoke singing, *everyone* has a chance to be a star. So why not put your best voice forward? If you're next in line to sing tonight, these pages will provide you with numerous, invaluable performance and singing tips to insure your moments in the spotlight are successful.

Keep this book with you wherever you go. Take whatever time is necessary to become familiar with its secrets. As you unlock your vocal resources, stage fright will turn into stage fun. If you're going to get up and sing, why not blow them away?

This Guide to **KARAOKE** Confidence will:

    ♪ ***PROVIDE HELPFUL INFORMATION ON HOW TO HANDLE PERFORMING ON STAGE.***

    ♪ ***EXPLAIN HOW TO OVERCOME STAGE FRIGHT.***

    ♪ ***ALLOW YOU TO SING BETTER IMMEDIATELY: GAIN POWER, CONFIDENCE, HIGH NOTES AND POISE .***

    ♪ ***EXPLAIN THE BASIC TECHNIQUES OF SINGING.***

    ♪ ***GIVE YOU THE PROFESSIONAL'S EDGE BY OUTLINING KEY "SECRETS OF SINGING" USED BY SINGERS WHO SET RECORDING INDUSTRY STANDARDS.***

There are definite do's and don'ts to sounding and looking at ease on the Karaoke stage. Along with reading this book, watch and listen to live, televised, or videotaped performances of singers you admire. Listen to as many recordings as you can in the style you want to sing. Studying great performers work will help you make sensible choices as to what does and what doesn't work on stage.

A practical, simple vocal technique is the foundation on which the emotional aspect of singing is built. If you attempt to pour out your soul before mastering some basics, you'll probably be asking yourself "Why doesn't my singing sound right?" or "Why don't I have fun when I get up to sing?"

A word of advice to all Karaoke singers: singing is the ultimate do-it-yourself activity. A little hard work and dedication can make your voice sound the way you want it to. Without some singing know-how, you'll be easily frustrated. Just liking to sing can quickly and easily be transformed into genuine singing confidence.

With this **KARAOKE** "crash course" and a willingness to practice these techniques, *you* will make a tremendous impression at your next Karaoke appearance.

If tonight's your night to go out on the town and sing with friends, family, or co-workers, read these simple guidelines and this time you'll be the star of the show!

PART 1:

LIVING COMFORTABLY ON STAGE

PART 1

BEYOND SINGING
IN THE SHOWER

Do you sing better in the shower than you do at a Karaoke club? Is your singing lively and enthusiastic at home, but stilted and uncomfortable in front of a crowd? Why is there such a big difference between singing for yourself versus singing for others?

Performing for an audience, rather than the tiles in your shower, is demanding. The presence of a crowd affects how you breathe, and how you look and act onstage. Singing is an activity that entails two-way communication. Your performance and voice stirs the audience, and they in turn respond to you. This is great when the audience is interested and shows enthusiasm for your singing. It's not so wonderful, however, when the audience seems unaffected by your performance.

But remember that it's two-way communication. The audience is responding to you. This means that in order to perform successfully, you've got to do your part.

A successful singing performance requires that you:

♪ Want to sing

♪ Have some basic stage presence skills

♪ Use some singing technique that works for you

♪ Want to share your feelings and your voice.

If you're not familiar with the typical Karaoke setting, the illustration below shows the usual layout. The key components you need to be acquainted with are the:

♪ microphone

♪ stage

♪ video monitor (or teleprompter) which displays the lyrics as you sing along with the music

♪ video camera

♪ Karaoke host's booth - where the accompaniment tapes are stored and played

♪ song list

♪ key-light - you want to stand in a part of the stage that's in the lights

♪ audience

FIGURE 3: Typical Karaoke Setup

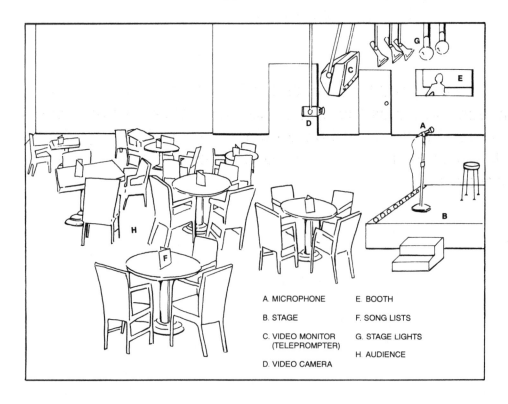

A. MICROPHONE

B. STAGE

C. VIDEO MONITOR (TELEPROMPTER)

D. VIDEO CAMERA

E. BOOTH

F. SONG LISTS

G. STAGE LIGHTS

H. AUDIENCE

DO'S AND DON'TS OF KARAOKE PERFORMING

No matter what you're singing, here are some basic performance guide-lines to get you started on the right track.

♪ Sing as if you were performing the song for the first time, not the hundredth.

♪ Make your performance worthy of the audience's time by getting the point or story of your song across.

♪ Show the audience that you enjoy singing and are happy to be performing for them.

♪ Acknowledge applause gracefully.

Above all, have a good time. Don't dwell on mistakes or your shortcomings. You can work on things that need improvement in your next practice session at home. But while onstage, keep focused on the things that are going right. Add excitement and passion to your performance by any reasonable means possible.

Avoid:

♪ Singing songs that are too difficult for you (at your present level).

♪ Boring the audience by singing a whole song in a monotone (the same vocal color).

♪ Hamming it up without really singing.

♪ Assuming that a good voice is all that's needed for a successful performance.

♪ Singing while slumped over the microphone staring at the floor.

FIGURE 4

KNOW THY SONG

At almost every Karaoke night spot, the words to the song you select are displayed on a monitor (a television which displays the lyrics). So it's really not necessary to memorize the songs you intend to sing. However, the more familiar you are with a song you intend to sing on any one night, the better. The best way to use the words on the monitor is as a backup, referring to them only now and then, rather than having to keep your eyes glued to them. When you don't need the monitor, you can *really* begin performing.

The best first step in preparing for your performance is to get acquainted with the song you want to sing. Singing requires a lot of control; the pitches of the melody, the lyrics, the rhythm, softs and louds, etc. have to be managed all at once. Performances improve to the degree that all this happens as routine rather than conscious effort. Ideally, it's best to have nothing to concentrate on but the song's meaning, emotion, and story line.

Before performing a song:

1. **Know the lyrics (words of a song).** As soon as possible, learn the lyrics almost by heart. Free yourself and your eyes to give in to the music and your audience.

2. **Try to select popular songs or those known as "standards."** Standards are musical compositions that have become familiar and are often performed over the years. They're likely to be in the collection of sing-along tapes maintained at the Karaoke club or restaurant.

In the case you want to sing a specialty song - one you wrote, a composition your own band sings (if you have one), or just something out of the ordinary - bring your own taped accompaniment. Inform the Karaoke host, who keeps the sign-up list for patrons wishing to sing that you have your own personal accompaniment. They'll be more than happy to play your tapes. This can be a nice change of pace for the audience and give you the comfort of knowing exactly how the accompaniment will sound.

3. **Practice speaking the lyrics meaningfully.** This will help to "set" the words in your mind. The better you can "say" your songs, the better you will sing them.

4. **Obtain a cassette that contains just the music.** This can be a simple piano accompaniment or a special cassette with music only and no singing purchased at a Karaoke store. Try speaking the lyrics along with the tape to get the feel of the rhythm. If you have trouble with the rhythm, clap it out until you have it memorized. These music-without-voice tapes can also be purchased at most music supply stores.

5. **Rehearse the melody.** Using an "AH" vowel only, sing the melody, in rhythm, along with your tape. If you have trouble with any segment of the song, take the difficult line and practice it slowly at first and then bring it up to speed. If a passage is particularly bothersome, use the techniques listed in **PART 2: THE VOCAL MAKEOVER** section to discover its probable cause and solution. Do this with all problem spots until you can sing through the entire song comfortably on just one vowel.

6. **Add the words**. Now add the lyrics, and again isolate and
practice any trouble spots.

After going through these steps, the lyrics, rhythm, melody and overall feel
of your song(s) should be so familiar that your musical selection practically
finds its way into your memory automatically.

When you know the song that you might sing on a Karaoke night out,
you've added a powerful advantage to your performance abilities. Free of
the monitor, you can open up to the audience and really deliver - rather
than just give a "reading" of your song.

CREATING "SINGERLY" LINES

One of the essential elements of successful singing is good phrasing. In a nutshell, it's what makes a voice sound **singerly** (you won't find this word in any dictionary - it's the author's own concoction).

When phrasing musically, your voice will seem smooth, pure, and well-controlled to your listeners.

EMPHASIZE VOWELS, DE-EMPHASIZE CONSONANTS

Competent singers move with tremendous agility through words all the while linking vowels (A,E,I,O, and U) as they smooth out the rough edges of consonants.

> ♪ By definition, a consonant is a sound (such as P, T,M, K, or S) produced by complete or partial blockage of the breath stream.

Singers we love to listen to time and time again gently tap consonants into words with the touch of a feather. But consonants are often the downfall of many Karaoke and would-be professional singers. Without careful handling of consonants, phrasing may bump along due to over-emphasizing their importance in the line of sung sounds.

If you've developed bad habits, such as:

> ♪ Allowing tension into the mouth or jaw area (your face turns into a grimace when singing), or

♪ If you sing with exaggerated pronunciation or seem to chew the words

then consonants are most likely taking over your singing with awkward phrasing the result.

Allow the last word of each sentence to act like a magnet pulling you along towards the next breath. Singing is not plodding along but moving through phrases keeping your performances alive and your audiences interested.

PASSION, YES;
OVERDOING IT, NO!

Sometimes, singers with the most passion are the ones who find the element of phrasing the most difficult. Why? Because they try **too hard**. Great singing sounds easy. Working on these secrets of singing will give your vocal performances polish and power.

But practice should _not_ be confused with overdoing it. Although quality practice time requires a certain heat or intensity to allow real work to be done, forcing the voice into compliance will never accomplish anything.

𝄞 In your practice sessions, you should always be relaxed and comfortable, allowing the tone to be as natural as possible. Then you can begin to define your "ideal" sound.

Often what happens when singers are overly concerned about "succeeding" in singing is that over-pronunciation dominates their speech patterns. As the consonants become larger and larger, vowels decrease in size until the throat locks up.

Generally, a little more emphasis (stretching out) of vowels and a little less stress on consonants turns choppy singing into "singerly" lines of tone. Don't confuse simple over-pronunciation with performing with true conviction and meaning.

GIVING LIFE TO YOUR PERFORMANCES

If you sing a Bette Midler song just like Bette, with all of her gestures, your audience will probably respond with a "not bad." However, if you sing a Bette Midler song with a conviction that this song is about <u>you</u>, *relating it to similar experiences or feelings from <u>your</u> life*, that's the stuff of exciting performances.

One of the most misunderstood aspects of performance is how to make a song your own. First, you need to pick a song which you relate to on an emotional level, and then personalize the lyrics.

After you're familiar with the lyrics, answer these questions:

🎼 Why did I choose to sing this song in the first place?

🎼 How does it relate to my life?

🎼 To whom am I singing this to? When you're on stage, if you can imagine singing the song to someone who has played a significant role in your life (good or bad), the audience members will think you're singing to them personally.

🎼 Do I know the story-line of my song? Songs are usually stories set to music. Certain tunes literally require you to tell the audience a story.

SEE YOURSELF IN THE SONG

A song will come alive for you and an audience when you're aware of the reasons for singing that particular song.

In every great interpretation of a song, there's a **need** for the singer to tell a particular story. <u>Before</u> getting up there at your next Karaoke performance, ask yourself, "why do <u>I</u> need, or want, to sing the song I've selected?" With the answer to this question clearly in mind, your singing will be full of life. ***Mean it when you sing it!*** You'll have the audience in the palm of your hands.

YOUR EYES TELL A STORY

Your eyes can be your greatest physical asset on stage, or your weakest. All singers struggle at one point or another with the questions, "Where should I look?" and "Should I make eye contact or look at the back wall, avoiding contact like the plague?"

To make sure your eyes and your voice are telling the same story, follow these simple guidelines:

Avoid:

♪ Gazing out into space, or looking down. This has the effect of making the audience feel they are being excluded from the performance. Looking down can make you seem embarrassed to be singing.

♪ Making intense, prolonged eye contact with members of the audience. People generally feel a bit confused and put on the spot by extended eye contact from a stranger singing on stage.

18

Don't let your eyes wander aimlessly around the room in which you're performing.

Do:

♪ Find several comfortable *spots* to focus your glance; preferably one on the left side of your audience, one on the right and one near the center. Include them all in your performance. If you're singing in a big room, this gives the audience members a feeling that you're taking them all into your performance (see Figure 6).

♪ Gaze just above, near or to the side of the eyes of any specific audience member that draws your attention. A *spot* can be any object, like a picture hanging on the wall, a light fixture, etc., you can comfortably rest your eyes on while singing.

Looking directly at someone can throw you off if you don't get the response you want.

FIGURE 6: Spotting the Eyes

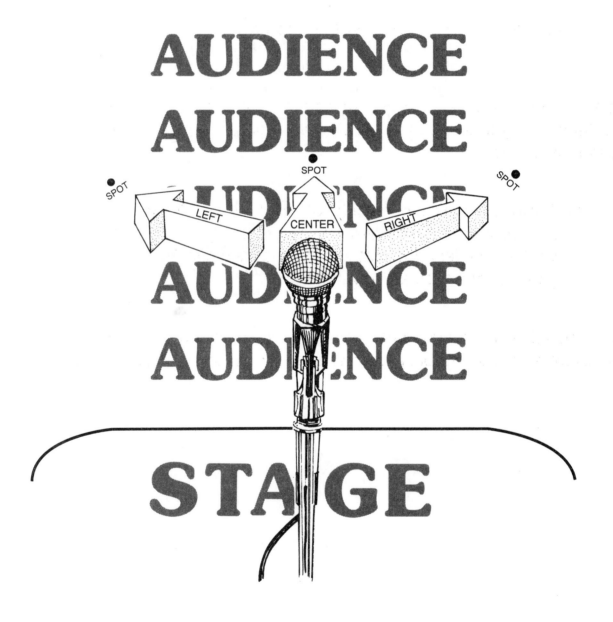

LOOKING GOOD ONSTAGE

Posture plays an important role in all of the performing arts, but especially in singing.

Good posture is crucial for effective breathing.

It's that simple. You can practice singing song after song until you're blue in the face, but you still won't acquire good breathing habits unless your posture is correct.

   ♯ Besides technical benefits of good posture, it also makes you look your best as you perform; it signals to your audience that you're confident and that you're not afraid to stand behind your performance and give it your all.

Some people come by good posture naturally. Many of us, however, need to pay attention to our habitual postures, and make adjustments, as necessary.

Posture is especially important for singers who are guitarists, bassists, drummers or pianists. Instrumentalists tend to fall into poor posture habits while practicing slumped over their instruments for hours on end.

Poor posture can lead to big singing problems. However, these problems often cease when you learn correct singing posture.

GOOD POSTURE ISN'T JUST STANDING UP STRAIGHT

When most people think about good posture, they think of "stomach in, chest out, shoulders back!" which is very rigid and tense. This kind of military posture will undermine your singing just as much as a slouched position.

So exactly what is the proper posture for singing? The right body set for you will be what feels comfortable and looks good. Because no one else has your bones and muscles, their way of standing won't necessarily be right for you.

By constantly experimenting with the position of your feet, shoulders, chest and head it is possible to arrive at a stance that will satisfy both you and your audience. For a complete rundown, from head to toe, of generally accepted characteristics of good posture, see figure 7 on the following page.

FIGURE 7: SINGING POSTURE

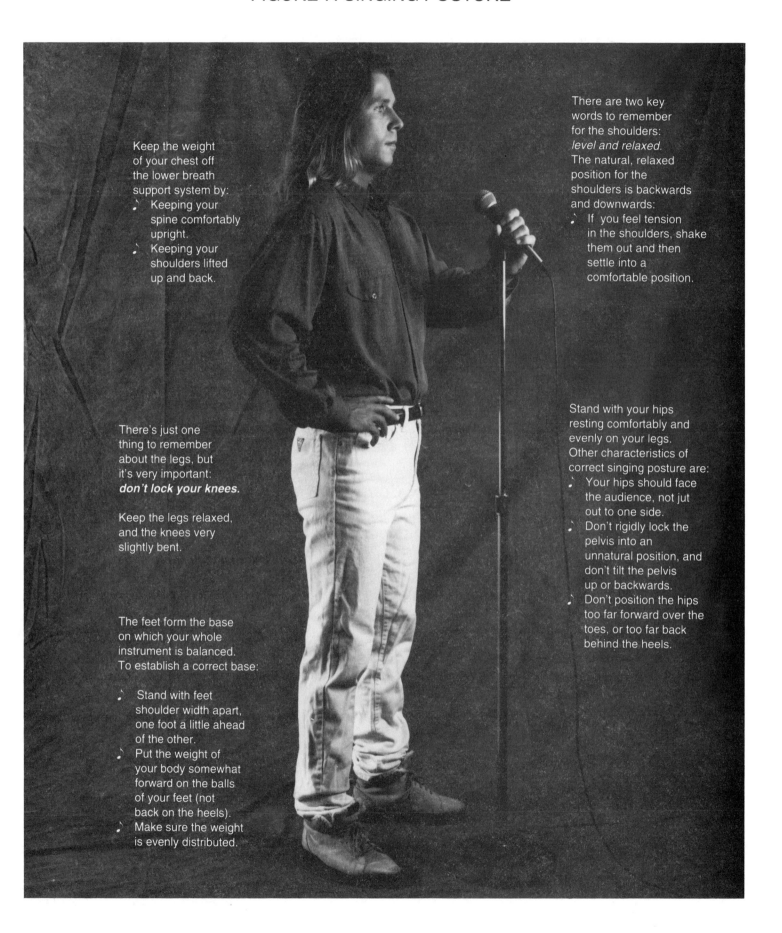

Keep the weight of your chest off the lower breath support system by:
- ♪ Keeping your spine comfortably upright.
- ♪ Keeping your shoulders lifted up and back.

There's just one thing to remember about the legs, but it's very important: **don't lock your knees.**

Keep the legs relaxed, and the knees very slightly bent.

The feet form the base on which your whole instrument is balanced. To establish a correct base:

- ♪ Stand with feet shoulder width apart, one foot a little ahead of the other.
- ♪ Put the weight of your body somewhat forward on the balls of your feet (not back on the heels).
- ♪ Make sure the weight is evenly distributed.

There are two key words to remember for the shoulders: *level and relaxed.* The natural, relaxed position for the shoulders is backwards and downwards:
- ♪ If you feel tension in the shoulders, shake them out and then settle into a comfortable position.

Stand with your hips resting comfortably and evenly on your legs. Other characteristics of correct singing posture are:
- ♪ Your hips should face the audience, not jut out to one side.
- ♪ Don't rigidly lock the pelvis into an unnatural position, and don't tilt the pelvis up or backwards.
- ♪ Don't position the hips too far forward over the toes, or too far back behind the heels.

STAYING LEVEL-HEADED ONSTAGE

The neck is one of the biggest problem areas for singers (both beginners and professionals) because it's particularly vulnerable to tension during performance.

What can you do to keep tension out of the neck area? One of the major keys to a relaxed neck is to keep your jaw line level (parallel to the ground).

Many performers lift or tilt their heads unconsciously, in an effort to avoid confronting the audience head-on (see Figure 8 below). This throws the entire natural vocal process out of alignment. Awkward head positions not only make singing difficult, but also give a strained look and sound to a performance. These awkward habits "telegraph" to the audience that you're not comfortable with the material you're singing.

FIGURE 8: Head Position

a) Too High   b) Correct   c) Too Low

BODY LANGUAGE

Keep in mind that the gesture or body language of your head counts. So try to sing with the head in a neutral position, neither too far up or too far down. This also alleviates the added tension on the voice box, which can result in a "pinched," cut-off tone. Furthermore:

- If your head is tilted too far up, you may seem aloof or haughty to the audience;

- If you slant your head too far down, you may be perceived as being somewhat embarrassed.

- Don't fall into the habit of looking down every time you breathe. Keep your head in position whether you're singing or breathing.

BE SPONTANEOUS

When performing, avoid pre-planning or "choreographing" your hand movements. Being spontaneous is easy to do when you've gained a few vocal skills, which enable you to put aside technical worries and deal with songs on an emotional level. When you're relaxed enough (due to gaining some singing confidence), your hands will automatically follow the feelings you express in your singing.

- More importantly, your hands convey feelings as a natural extension of your performing style.

Unforced gestures make for an honest and unique performance. It's far better to express yourself in that way than insert pre-programmed gestures into your act. Once you're "in" a song emotionally, your voice and body will follow with natural, easy movements.

FIGURE 9

BUILDING CONFIDENCE

The singers that Karaoke audiences find enjoyable, have developed a high degree of poise (literally defined as "a stable, balanced state"). Many people think that these performers are different than the rest of us. The truth is that you don't have to be born with poise, it can be developed.

In fact, first rate Karaoke singers often times have private dress rehearsals <u>at home first</u> of the song, or songs, they intend to sing before audiences. You should, too. These in-home performances provide a time to check your posture, face, mannerisms, and hand gestures in a full-length mirror while singing the song as you're going to sing it at the Karaoke club.

Make sure that you're not frowning or grimacing, or making awkward gestures. Try out the clothes you're going to wear on stage ahead of time to make sure they don't inhibit your breathing and are comfortable to sing in. If you see yourself doing something you don't like, fix it or delete it from your performance. Trust yourself and a close friend or relative on these matters.

If a gesture or habit disturbs you a little at home, it will bother the audience a lot when you're onstage. *Less is usually more onstage.*

And last, but not least, it's critical to concentrate on your love of the music. Your goal is to enjoy singing onstage, even though there will always be room for improvement. Learn to enjoy singing as a process, rather than expecting a perfect performance every time. ***Singers who show a sense of delight and sincerity in performing never fail to engage their audience.***

FIGURE 10

CONQUERING STAGE FRIGHT

If you're still a bit nervous about singing in front of a crowd (or a single person, for that matter), join the club. However, don't make the assumption, as many singer/performers do, that stage fright is incurable. Quite the contrary.

The first step in managing stage fright is to establish pre-performance habits that calm nervousness. It bares repeating that you should always try to:

♪ **Choose a song** appropriate for your level of vocal abilities.

♪ **Be very familiar** with the lyrics of your song choices.

♪ **Isolate any difficult passages** and practice them ahead of time until you're comfortable singing the entire song.

♪ **Sing at every opportunity**. In time, experience will relieve you of jangled nerves. The more you get up before people and sing, the easier it becomes.

If you have nagging doubts such as "will I make the upcoming top note?" or "will I get the timing right on this phrase?" these questions will loom even larger in your mind when singing onstage. Lay these concerns to rest before you perform by selecting material you're comfortable with, and (I can't stress this enough) put in some practice time at home.

Yes, practice the song (or songs) you intend to perform. A little rehearsing goes a long way to increasing your confidence level. Here are some other issues a little practice can help you manage effectively:

🎼 **Subconscious fears and doubts.** Stage fright can be calmed by remembering that the audience accepts your best effort unconditionally and will be thrilled anytime you do your best and are sincere.

🎼 **Physical tension.** You can learn to counteract physical tension in a variety of ways. One of the quickest and most effective techniques is to get a firm grasp on your breathing.

🎼 **Learn to breathe low and quietly (as described in PART 2: THE VOCAL MAKEOVER).** Low silent breathing will steady the voice. This simple adjustment will help bring the rest of the nervous system under control.

🎼 **The awareness of your nervousness.** It's not really the symptoms of nervousness that are so terrible. It's the emotion itself. If you dwell on the fear, it starts a self-defeating cycle.

♪ To distract yourself from the fear of nervousness felt on stage when about to sing, concentrate on what you're going to do with the song as you sing it for the audience, not on how you're feeling.

♪ When you catch yourself thinking about how afraid you are, re-direct your energy to your breathing, or the lyrics.

If your mind wanders back to your nervousness (which it may, in the beginning), keep bringing your focus back to the controllable factors that will enhance your performance.

♪ Check your posture.
♪ Locate the spots in the room where you might focus your eyes.
♪ Re-involve yourself in what your song means to you.

USE YOUR JITTERS TO JUMPSTART YOUR PERFORMANCE

Don't lose sight of the fact that performing almost always has an element of nervous tension. When under control, your nervousness will literally be transformed into "passion." This is, in fact, a necessary ingredient of every satisfying performance.

Experienced singers, by practicing the techniques mentioned above, learn to use this nervous edge to their advantage - adding excitement to their performance. All singers, professionals as well as amateurs, get nervous. Successful singers, through experience, simply learn how to keep on singing in spite of their nerves. *You can too!*

THE MICROPHONE

If you haven't done a lot of performing, chances are the microphone may be a bit intimidating. Actually, as your performance experience increases you'll soon agree that a microphone is a singer's best friend. It allows you to be heard in every corner of the room, gives one of your hands something to do and provides a target where you can "aim" or "focus" the voice (more on this in **PART 2**).

There really aren't a lot of rules to using the "mic." The most difficult thing will probably be getting used to hearing the sound of your voice amplified (and seeing yourself plastered all over the club on the various television monitors and big screen TVs if your club shoots video during the performances).

But that's all part of the fun! It's you bigger than life, and there's only one you, so make the most of it. The fact that you're unique automatically makes you of great interest to the audience.

When using a microphone:

   ♪ Don't clutch the microphone with a strangle hold. This is popular among rock musicians, however, the tension of grasping the "mic" will cause the muscles in your shoulders and neck to tense.

   ♪ Sing <u>at</u> the "mic," and imagine projecting your sound to fill the entire room in front of you.

   ♪ Don't point the microphone at the ceiling. Instead, keep the microphone pointed at your mouth - *slightly below and in front of your chin.* This will also prevent it from covering up your face.

FIGURE 11: Holding the microphone;

A. Too high   B. Correct   C. Too low

Don't put your mouth on the microphone. You don't know where that microphone has been. It may be very dirty. Even more importantly, if it's not wired correctly, it can give you an electric shock on the lips. Keep a healthy distance (a few inches at least) away from the head of the microphone. Don't "kiss the mic," as an old stage saying goes, unless it's your own.

On higher or louder notes, pull the microphone away from your mouth.

On low or soft tones, move the microphone in closer to your lips so it can pick up the subtler shades of your singing.

LAST MINUTE PREPARATIONS

While you're waiting to go up and sing, the biggest challenge is to stay calm, cool and collected. In the typical Karaoke setup, you look through one or more song books or wall charts of the songs available. Then you tell the "DJ", or Karaoke host, who is working the playback equipment, which song you want to sing, and when your name is called, go up to the microphone.

To guarantee success in your next Karaoke performance consider these simple preparations:

1. **Be sure you've selected your song in advance.** Check the lists usually available from the sound source operator responsible for playing your accompaniment tape. Most established Karaoke clubs and restaurants have pamphlets listing songs in their library waiting for you on the tables. Don't let this decision wait until the last minute. Know what your intended song is and be sure it's available before going up on stage to avoid last minute confusion.

2. **Sip some room temperature water while you wait to sing.** Keeping the voice hydrated is like maintaining the proper amount of oil in your car. (Ice water is a bit shocking to the vocal cords.)

3. **Work on yourself until you find that _inner_ smile.** By this I mean you'll want to be engaging and pleasant to look at when performing your song. The first step in this regard is to get your head in a good place. Forget any problems at work or home and get involved with your friends, other audience members and the surroundings. Have fun!

4. **Go over the lyrics.** Run through the imagery in your head before going on stage to give your performance. Remember to sing the song for the members of the audience, as well as for yourself.

5. **Quiet yourself.** Take in the room around you, become familiar with your surroundings. Pay attention to your breathing, etc. Use any technique that works for you to calm and center yourself.

6. **Try singing songs recognized by the audience as made famous by the <u>opposite</u> sex.** It's less likely you'll be compared to the original artist.

7. **Women** - if you choose songs originally recorded and made famous by men, they'll always be in a comfortably low key.

8. **Men** - be careful about singing songs originally recorded by women. You'll probably end up singing the song much higher or lower than is comfortable. If you wish to "cover" (that is, sing a song made famous by a popular artist) a ladies' song, bring your own accompaniment tape in a suitable key.

9. **Avoid singing the most popular songs currently being played on the radio or in music videos.** This helps to avoid the inevitable comparisons to a superstar's famous version.

10. **Don't abuse alcoholic beverages.** No one wants to see a singer whose gestures and voice are out of control. Don't make the mistake of thinking the audience will be interested or sympathetic to such behavior.

PART 2:

THE VOCAL MAKEOVER:
TIPS, TRICKS AND SECRETS OF SINGING

FIGURE 12

INTRODUCTION

There are four aspects of vocal technique that work together to make singing feel comfortable to you and enjoyable to your audience. These are:

- Breath support and control
- Mouth position
- Focus
- Anchoring Tone

Understanding how to gain control of each instrumental part and how they work together will help your singing enormously. Many vocal problems that take away from your sense of confidence can be quickly changed just by understanding a little bit about how the voice works.

One of the most common beliefs held by part-time singers is that the voice is completely formed in the throat, at the site of the vocal cords. This is far from the total picture. As you'll see in the following pages, there are actually many essentials that combine to form your "voice."

BREATHING FOR SINGERS: QUICK AND SIMPLE

The foundation of all singing is breathing. **Singing requires a strong, controlled breathing system.**

When taking a breath for singing:

1. Breathe from the bottom of your lungs up, just as you fill a cup when you pour yourself a glass of water.

FIGURE 13: Filling Lungs From the Bottom Up

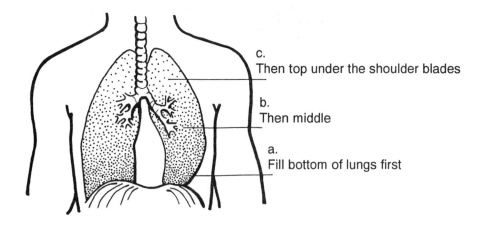

c.
Then top under the shoulder blades

b.
Then middle

a.
Fill bottom of lungs first

40

🎼 When breathing properly, you'll be able to feel the breath bypass your upper chest, resulting in a *360 degree stretch around your lower abdomen*, not just in front.

🎼 The upper chest or shoulders may lift as you're practicing the singing breath. ***Don't let this happen!***

2. Check to make sure that you're breathing properly.

🎼 Place the web (between the index finger and thumb) of your hands in the soft spot between the ribs and hip bones on both sides of your body.

🎼 Rest your fingertips on your stomach and your thumbs on the small of your back (see Figure 14). As you inhale, the gathering breath should cause your thumb and fingertips to stretch apart.

Figure 14: Checking The Singing Breath

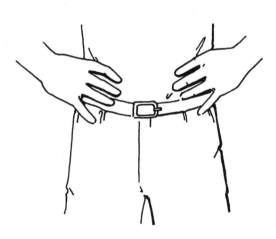

3.   *Breathing that fills the lower abdomen first and then expands up under the upper ribs and shoulder blades is the key.* For most people, this will feel quite different from their normal breathing. Why? Because most of us go through the day taking very shallow breaths.

This can be caused by stress or simply allowing lazy living habits to overtake our daily routine.

MOUTH VS. NOSE BREATHING

Many singers wonder "Should I breathe through my nose or my mouth?"

Mouth breathing is preferable because:

- It helps you get a good stretch in the lower breath support muscles;

- You'll achieve the feeling of storing the breath low in the lungs.

In the final analysis, mouth vs. nose breathing is a highly personal matter. Whichever you choose, be sure that each breath is *low, quiet, and helps you feel relaxed and ready to sing.* Some singers actually successfully breathe through both at the same time. Do whatever feels natural to you.

BREATH SUPPORT AND CONTROL: OPPOSITES BUT EQUAL

If you really want to build vocal power, you've got to gain breath support *and* control. They go hand in hand. They're also exact opposites.

♪ ***Breath support*** refers to the upward action of your tummy or abdominal muscles when singing. These are the same muscles developed when you do sit-ups or leg-lifts (a recommended activity for singers, I might add). These lower support muscles powerfully, yet slowly, cause air to be moved up through the instrument.

A common tendency is to yank in the tummy while singing which forces too much air to hit the cords. The vocal cords will, if allowed, automatically take the amount of air that they need. In fact, when correct breathing habits are in place, a simple sip of air, rather than a large gulp, brings in more than enough air to sing. As a singer, your job is to gently breathe in a small amount of air. Your voice itself will take care of returning air up to the cords with just the right amount of power.

If you can hear yourself gasping for air every time you breathe while singing, you're taking in too much air. Take quiet breaths, never gasp!

𝄞 **_Breath control_** refers to how much air you can keep *away* from the cords. More specifically, it refers to how effectively the diaphragm (the main muscle of breath control) resists the belly muscles as they press air up to the vocal cords. Too much air moving into the cords at any one time can cause the voice to unexpectedly crack.

FIGURE 15 A & B: Showing the Position of the Diaphragm at Rest (Before Inhalation) and then During Inhalation and while Singing

a) At Rest

b) Positioned for Inhalation and Control

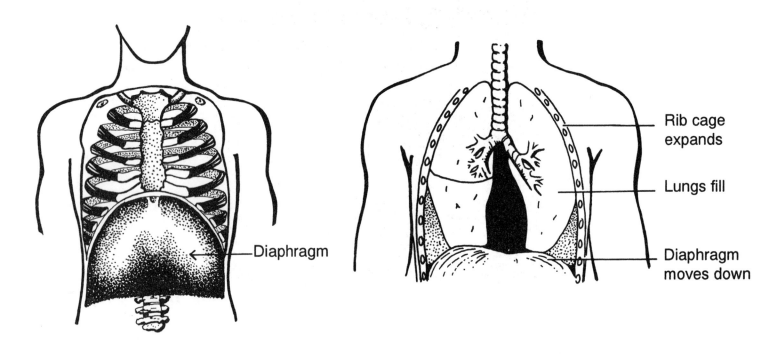

Diaphragm

Rib cage expands

Lungs fill

Diaphragm moves down

THE OLD BELT TRICK

Here's a helpful secret you can use at your next Karaoke performance to be sure your breathing is right on the mark.

1. Hitch a belt or elastic band around your waist at the exact location indicated in FIGURE 16.

FIGURE 16: Correct Location of Belt

2. Tighten the belt so it's comfortably snug and when you breathe, it stretches outwards.

♪ Keep the belt in this manner underneath whatever shirt or top you wear to a Karaoke club or restaurant.

♪ Hidden in this way, the belt (or band) will serve as a reminder to breathe low and not force too much air into the cords.

3.   With each breath you take for your song, the belt should *gently* stretch outward.

4.   While singing, gently continue the outwards stretch of your lower ribs, back and tummy against the belt. As these muscles are all attached to the diaphragm, this action will help it to "sit on the upcoming air" so to speak and resist against the power provided by the lower support muscles.

The feeling of breath control is similar to the downward flexing motion used when having a bowel movement or even comparable to the sensation of bearing down to birth a baby.

Use the belt trick until you're confident about getting a good low breath every time you breathe for singing. The audience won't know your secret, but your poise and power will improve a hundred-fold. Low breathing is the number one antidote to nervousness!

When pressing air up to the cords or resisting to control this breath, never allow the muscles to become rigid. Firm but flexible is enough to get the job done. As the feelings of belly muscles pressing up for support and the diaphragm leaning down and away (from the lungs) become equal, breath will be at your service.

Controlled breath support will give you the uncanny sensation of air gently falling backwards towards the bottom of your throat while singing. Pushing (yelling) occurs when air is simply shoved out of the lungs without any control whatsoever.

A VOCAL STATE OF MIND

Many singers have an incomplete understanding of what happens to air once it leaves the vocal cords. The pathway breath follows from the cords to the outside world is extremely important in singing. The more clearly you can visualize this pathway, the better you'll sing.

THE PERFECT MODEL: A BASEBALL PITCH

Study the illustration below carefully. The perfect shape to imagine when you're singing is like that described by the pitcher's arm in the illustration below. Think about what the arm movement of a good baseball pitch looks like: the pitcher's arm swings back, up, and finally forward.

FIGURE 17: Baseball Pitch

♯ Imagining a similar arching pathway for vibrating air (after it moves through the vocal cords) while singing accomplishes the following:

♪ It frees the voice by insuring the roof of the mouth is raised and the back of the throat open.

♪ Allows sound to amplify in the vast network of sinuses and resonating spaces above the throat, behind the nose, and in the forehead.

By just imagining the pathway correctly (see Figure 18 below), the voice will begin to brighten and become much more flexible. The voice seems to float, detached and weightless, moving out to the audience along the pathway.

If you can imagine a pathway with enough arch, even the highest notes of your voice will come within reach.

FIGURE 18: Imagery-Pathways of Tone

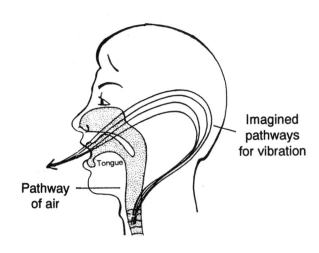

MOUTH POSITION: OPEN UP AND SAY AH...

Finding a beneficial mouth position is largely dependent on the position of the jaw. When singing, the mouth should move towards an oval shape with the corners drawn in and the jaw *gently* let down.

🎼 Singing becomes difficult when the jaw:

♪ is dropped rigidly
♪ is drawn backwards too forcibly
♪ juts forward with undue effort

FIGURE 19: Mouth Position (Correct and Incorrect)

a) Correct	b) Incorrect
Correct mouth position = focused tone	Incorrect mouth position = no focus

OPEN UP THE THROAT
WITH A BIT OF A YAWN

To further open up the back of the throat, create the feeling of the <u>beginning</u> of a yawn. This slightly yawned position opens up some space between the back molars allowing for the critical link between the resonances of the head and lower throat and chest.

🎼 A bit of a yawn also readies the pathway and improves the tongue position.

🎵 Remember, only add the *beginning* of a yawn. If you activate the feeling of a big yawn, rather than freeing the voice, you'll create a new barrier in the pathway.

Any time your song requires that you hold a tone for 2 - 5 seconds, imagine the sensation of the beginning of a yawn (as the tone is sustained) to help maintain an open throat.

INNER MOUTH POSITION

A major source of potential trouble in the mouth area is the tongue. Be sure the tip of your tongue lies relaxed against the back of your bottom front teeth when you sustain a tone for a long time.

FIGURE 20: Tongue Positions

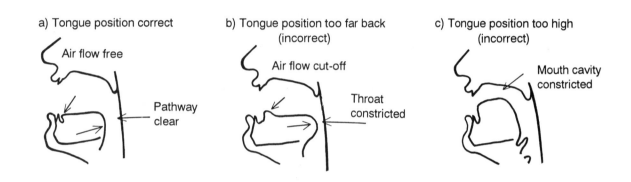

This isn't to say that the tongue doesn't move up, back and all around the mouth as you form words while singing.

  ♪ However, when the tongue lifts too far up, or pulls back, it separates the mouth into two separate resonators, front and back, cutting off the tone.

  ♪ When rehearsing songs, it's a good idea to use a hand-held mirror to check that your tongue is comfortably forward when singing (extended tones).

The parts of the mouth continuously move to fine-tune the oral cavity until the feel and sound of any tone is just right. The tongue, jaw and mouth in general are not held rigidly, but must be free relaxed if tone is to be pleasing to your audience.

POWER UP WITH FOCUS

Air and vibration, at the end of the arching journey through the throat and mouth, must be given a final enhancement known as "point", "edge", "ring", or *"focus."*

Like the proverbial pot of gold at the end of the rainbow, the vocal pathway ends in one of the richest sources of vocal power.

🎼 Focus assures a comfortable singing tone, that carries or projects the voice well as it leaves the pathway.

🎼 Focus gives vocal tone more brilliance and smooths out the rough edges.

Focus is achieved when the voice is free to move up through an open mouth and throat to enter the upper resonators in the nasal passages, cheek bones and forehead. Together these areas of tonal amplification are known as the *mask*.

FIGURE 21: The Mask

THINKING LIKE A SINGER

You may be wondering at this point how to achieve focus. Part of this is done automatically via the mouth shaping as described in the mouth position section. It's also helpful to use some proven mental imagery to control the inner workings of the voice. The next time you sing:

♪ Imagine a wall one to two feet in front of you, between you and your audience (see FIGURE 22).

♪ Now, visualize a small hole-in-the-wall about the size of a quarter and a little below the level of your mouth .

♪ Imagine your voice soaring back, up and over along the pathway, coming out of your mouth and then moving through the hole-in-the-wall to the audience.

FIGURE 22: Aiming Air Through
The Hole-In-The-Wall

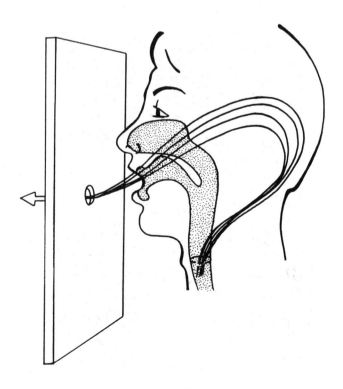

Just thinking of aiming the voice through a small hole in an imaginary wall will affect the muscles of the throat, causing them to consolidate the air into a more ringing sound.

You aim the air the same as you would aim a dart at a target. Knowing that you want to hit the bulls-eye, you visualize where the bull's eye is and then direct your arm to throw the dart towards it.

Mentally, do the same with the voice. After releasing your voice back (to fill the space opened up by the yawn), up and over along the pathway, aim it through the hole-in-the-wall. Tone focused in this manner is picked up by a microphone more effectively. In fact, when singing at your Karaoke nightclub or restaurant, place your "focal point" (the hole-in-the-wall) on the head of the microphone you're singing into.

FIGURE 23: Focusing the Voice on the Microphone

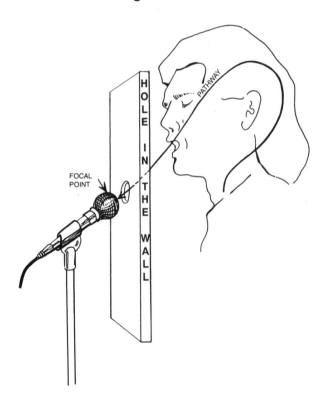

The voice is released back onto the pathway and aimed forward through the hole-in-the-wall simultaneously. This insures all upper and middle resonators—head, mouth and throat are included in your singing.

AUTOMATIC VS. STICKSHIFT:

(BLENDING VOCAL COLORS)

In addition to the vocal characteristics of the head, mouth and throat resonators, powerful singing also involves a third tonal quality that comes from the bones and cavities of the chest. Thus, the voice has three major sources of vocal resonance or amplification: the head (upper resonance), the mouth (middle resonance), and the throat and chest (lower resonance).

To achieve a balanced tone, singers learn to keep these vocal colors mixed together. Top-notch vocalists release vocal tone which they *feel* high in the head, forward in the mouth, low in the throat and deep in the chest *all at the same time.*

FIGURE 24: Location of Various
Resonation Zones

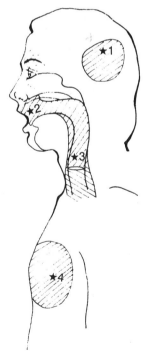

1. ★ High in the Head
2. ★ Forward in the Mouth
3. ★ Low in the Throat
4. ★ Deep in the Chest

ANCHORING TONE

The key secret to blending these resonances is to realize the mouth, lying right smack in between the head and throat/chest resonators is the perfect "mixer" for tone.

🎼 The mouth receives tone from both upper and lower resonators, and *anchors,* or centers it, giving it the balance required for truly expressive singing.

A key to blending is to always keep the mouth full of vowel, vibration, or tone.

When your tone is anchored, you'll have the sensation that your mouth is full of whatever vowel sound you're singing. It'll feel so tangible, that you'll feel as if you could almost chew the vowel sound!

🎼 Ring or brilliance from the mask (found through using proper mouth position and focusing imagery) combines with deep tones from the bottom of the throat and chest to fill the mouth.

A well-anchored tone gains the quality of depth by vibrating all the way down to the bottom of your chest, and attains brilliance as it rings throughout your head. When your mouth feels alive with vibration from your chest, throat, mouth, and head, you're anchored (see FIGURE 25 on the next page).

🎼 In fact, the whole body feels connected to your tone when the voice is truly ringing out.

♪ Under optimum conditions, it seems like the mouth is so filled with vibration that when you open it, the vibrating tone will virtually overflow out to the admiring audience.

That's how simple singing should become. You open up the mouth and let out the vibration gathering there from the resonators above and below. *The various resonators of the body are the head, mouth, throat and chest. Your voice must not be stationed in any **one** of these sources of vocal power, but ring from all four at once.*

Singers who concentrate on filling their mouths with tone and then filling the rooms around them always sing more confidently. When you fill your biggest resonator (the mouth) to the brim, then project the tone mentally along the pathway to the imaginary hole-in-the-wall, the room around you will fill as well.

FIGURE 25: Anchored and Double-Anchored Tone

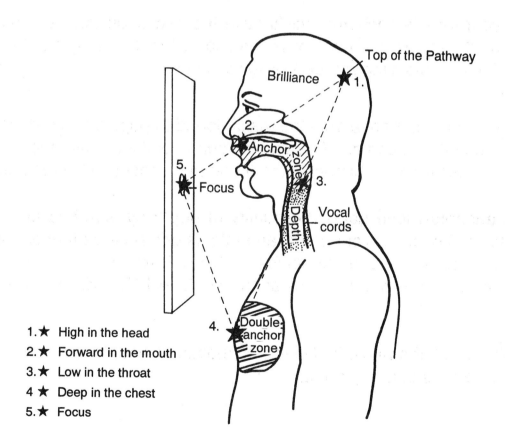

1.★ High in the head
2.★ Forward in the mouth
3.★ Low in the throat
4 ★ Deep in the chest
5.★ Focus

In the upper range, an important image and sensation to strive for is the voice leaning (or vibrating) right on your breastbone, sternum, and chest in general. A *double-anchored* effect results when the brilliance of high notes is first rounded and mixed with deeper tone colors in the mouth, and then stabilized by resting or rooting in the depths of the chest itself.

The illustration on the previous page shows the two anchoring zones (mouth and chest) as well as their relationship to the focal point and top of the pathway.

To double-anchor a top note one imagines the support muscles pressing breath right onto the inside wall of the chest before it leap-frogs up the pathway and out through the nose and mouth. Tone seems to spring from the mask, mouth and chest simultaneously when well anchored.

"The ideal tone, is a mouthful of sound that 'spins,' remolds itself for every vowel, is felt at the lips, in the head, presses down the tongue, pushes up the [roof of the mouth], even descends into the chest, in fact fills every nook and cranny ."
Giovanni Battista Lamperti

PLACEMENT: SINGING WITH A FULL DECK OF CARDS

Placement is one of those musical terms just vague enough to be confusing. What it actually describes is the balance of resonance that occurs between the lower and upper tone qualities.

If your tone is emphasizing upper or head resonance, the voice is said to be "placed" high or forward. On the other hand, if your lower resonators, the throat and chest, are mostly coloring the tone, placement is said to be "low," "down," or even sometimes "further back."

𝄞 Where you choose to emphasize or concentrate the energy of the voice depends on what mood you want to convey.

Placement is one of the most important ingredients of expression. It gives variety to your singing.

HOW TO CREATE A MOOD BY PLACING YOUR VOICE

Though an oversimplification, you could say that to express a happy, light feeling, you would place the voice by leaning it more into the mask area.

Darker, somber moods are revealed by allowing the tone to develop more in the lower throat and chest.

The key is to remember that the voice, while anchored in the mouth, partakes of some degree of upper and lower qualities at all times.

A subtle emphasis, or mental leaning, of the voice into either mask or towards throat and chest resonance is all that's necessary to infuse tone with many of the emotional colors at your command.

FIGURE 26: Placing the Voice to
Convey Specific Feelings

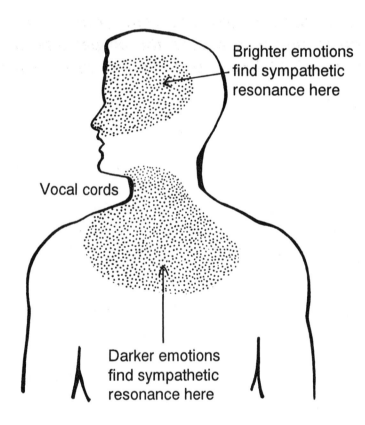

All of these adjustments can occur automatically, just by knowing the mood or quality of sound you want to make.

If you consistently practice and master the basics of singing, placement takes care of itself. This is especially true if you have your emotional intention clearly in mind before you start singing a song.

The better you can imagine how you want your singing to sound, the more automatically the voice blends the proper amount of upper and lower resonances - just like it does when you express yourself in speech.

NEVER FEAR HIGH NOTES
AGAIN

A note is a note: no more, no less.

To produce clear, ringing "high" notes, you only need to remember the basics of good tone production:

♪ Breathe into and press (support) from the lower muscles (front, sides, and back).

♪ "Sit on the air" or resist down and out with the diaphragm for control. Try to breathe in and sing with as little air as possible.

♪ Yawn a bit, relax the jaw.

♪ Conceive any top note as a mouthful of vowel that is simultaneously felt high on the pathway, forward in the mouth, deep in the throat and low in the chest.

When you achieve this combination of feelings, all "high" notes will seem as easy to sing as the middle notes. This is especially true when performing songs that leap to a high note or when starting a phrase on a high pitch.

The secret to singing high notes is to sing them in exactly the same way as you sing tones in the lower portion of your voice. Powerful, ringing high notes are anchored in the mouth and then (via a throat loosened up with a bit of yawn) allowed to vibrate down to resonate or double-anchor in the chest.

By aiming top notes down and out to the hole-in-the-wall along the pathway, they will stay firmly in the ringing bones of the head and focused. This practice will stop the tendency to reach (literally crane your head and neck up) for top tones. Keeping non-essential air away from the cords is important and will also prevent you from smacking top notes with too much air.

KEEP SINGING!

Now that you've gained access to the world of vocal know-how, you're probably wondering how to get even more serious about voice training. Step up to the ultimate manual of voice strengthening and maintenance, Jeffrey Allen's *Secrets of Singing*®. This landmark training manual for singers is quickly becoming a staple at many top music schools and universities. In it you'll find nearly four hundred pages of easy to read, practical information and over one hundred illustrations, charts and photographs on the art of singing.

If you're determined to become a singer or need to improve your current abilities, *Secrets of Singing's* cutting edge techniques and proven procedures will allow you to stand out from the crowd and make your dreams a reality.

FIGURE 27